ALL THIS REMAINS TO BE DISCOVERED

Sandra de Helen

TABLE OF CONTENTS

INTRODUCTION

This collection is intended as a memoir of sorts,
but some people already believe all poetry is
memoir already. So there you are, forewarned. As
my friend, poet Ginny Foster often said, all life is
grist for the mill. We write what we know, and we
often grind up our memories, our feelings, our
friends' stories, our lover's hearts, any thing that
crosses our path into our own stories or poems.

What I have found in my own life and practice of
writing is that the first times I write about a
memory it may be painful and the anger or hurt
shows up on the page. By the third or thirtieth
time I write about the incident I may have started
to soften enough to add forgiveness to the mix. In
this way, I hope the people who read my work or
who hear me read my work find something that
resonates. Whether that is the anger or the
forgiveness depends on where they are in their
own process. That is not my business.

Thank you for taking time to read or listen to my
words. Please know that though I wrote about my
mother at her worst here, she and I had many long
conversations over the years, and I know she
always did the best she could do, as we all do. She
loved me, and I loved her. sdh

DISCOVERING CHILDHOOD

WEDNESDAY'S CHILD

Born in mid-week, I got a
late start. Mom asked
nurse why I had dark circles
under my eyes. Didn't she
realize how much I had to do
in this life and it was already
Wednesday? No time for lying
around cooing and eating
there was work to be done.
I didn't walk until she gave
me shoes, but I painted the
kitchen floor at nine months.
I saw a brush and a can of
paint and the floor was what
I could reach. At two I helped
plant the vegetable garden by
picking up beans she was
"dropping" in rows. As she
took them from her bucket
and placed them on the
ground, I picked them up
and placed them in my
own bucket. At three I was
stringing beans, hulling peas
and stemming huckleberries.
At four I learned to read and
tell time, fold the laundry, and
mop on my hands and knees.
By five I was washing dishes,
sweeping, changing the baby's
diaper, and rocking her to sleep.
School was a welcome respite.
Wednesday's child is said to
be full of woe, but that is not
my nature. Maybe I was actually
due on Saturday and got to
work early.

NOW WE ARE SIX

Your faded blue cover is covered
in line drawings of Pooh and
friends. They are my friends too,
my Nanny, my
doctor who cures sneezles
and wheezles, my good King
John. My favorites are the racing
raindrops, but we are in a seven-year drought,
whatever that means, so no raindrops here.
I look for city beetles to
put in matchboxes, but
we live in the country.
I find garter snakes.
They don't like matchboxes,
and I don't have
Nanny, I have Mama
who doesn't cotton to
critters in matchboxes,
or in the house at all.
Your pages are soft and thick
as diapers, of which we have plenty —
they go with the baby
I prayed for every night
on my knees. I thought
she would play, but she
can't even read. So
I read to her from the
pages that are whole,
saving the torn ones
for myself. They're secret
code pages from before. I'm still
working out the meaning.
I mean, everybody knows no one
tears pages in books for no reason,
so I'm working out the code. The mystery
only I can solve.

WHAT MOM SAID TO MY SISTER

When will you ever grow up
and stand on your own two feet?
Drinking milk from a 7-Up bottle
whose idea was that?
Can't you eat something besides
mashed potatoes for a year?
You're nothing but skin and
bones and your hair needs a
good combing. Come back here.
I heard you were out smoking
behind the propane tank, is
that true? Didn't think so.
Who ever heard of a seven year
old smoking? No, your sister
didn't tattle on you. Your friend's
sister. I didn't believe her.
Now get in there and eat
something for once in your
life. No, there ain't no more
mashed potatoes. You'll just
have to eat some toast.
Ask your sister to open the
jelly. I gotta go to work.

SISTER

For you I always wear cashmere
come bearing gifts
pick up the check
have all the answers
and never say no.
You got damned tired
of that persona about
fifty years ago, and yet
we both hang onto her
sometimes when you need
your milk in a 7-Up bottle
or I want to feel I have some
control over my life
or we're on our way to Jack's
Drugstore, which is long gone
except in our minds, and
we just want a little piece
of down home comfort.
Then we stop for a cup
of tea and you pick up
the check and I don't
wear a sweater 'cause
it's the fifth of July and
I've never had all the
answers anyway, and
no one has control over
her life ever really. But
I'm glad I'm your sister
and I'm glad you're my
sister, and I'm glad
we have each other,
and if you ever want
your milk in a 7-Up
bottle, I'm your gal.

TREE HOUSE

Huckleberry raft fifteen feet above
rusty red swing set, The Well of Loneliness
my pillow and only companion,
I gaze another fifty feet upwards
through chartreuse leaves
into July sky, waiting for daylight.
Dew chills my body clad in uniform
of shorts and camp shirt,
my brown feet bare.

My final season of innocence,
I neither know nor care.
Floating in bliss and daydreams,
so grandly above my daily life,
is it any wonder I reflect
on that sanctuary,
as I have throughout
the fifty years
spanning then and now?

The river propelled me from
American Sycamore
over the dams and canyons –
dry beds, floods, rapids,
and water moccasin snakes –
carried me on a raft
of my own making,
a branch barely able to keep me
afloat at times. Not the sturdy
floor in my playhouse with its
spiky round seed heads and
peeling arms that held me safe
my summer of content.

DISCOVERING THE TEEN YEARS

CADILLAC CONFESSIONAL

Forgive me for being twelve,
blond, a good kid, a bad
reporter. The front seat
will no more keep
its quiet, the rest stop refuses
any longer to withhold
its brutal secrets from
our hearts. I fell for
the fifty-year-old American
Shriner who
gives rides.

I've invoked the goddess.
I've desecrated – no – I
flamencoed at the cemetery
that led to fiery tap-dancing.
With crows'
raucous applause.

A breast
touching arm, the tongue
hooked inside teeth.
I'll get over it and
bring myself about all over
again: the predatory American
the   groping banker

with the freckled hands. But
I'll not cry tears
dripping someone else's salt.
At twelve, I was wizened
by a Shriner of fifty
in the oversized
celadon Cadillac
out past
Rolla.

My mother
shamed me into accepting
the fiver.

I could die.

THAT ORANGE AND WHITE SKIRT

… I wore that night was one of
my favorites. It was a houndstooth
check. I love houndstooth checks.
Orange and white. No one else had
one like it. It fit me great too.
I didn't have to hide my stomach.
I could tuck in my blouse. Wear
my bobby socks rolled down.
Elvis was on Ed Sullivan that
night for the second time. Mom
let me go up to Ronnie's house
with Carol and Butch and we
watched it with Ronnie and his
mom and granddad. Carol and I
were writhing around, but not
screaming. Ronnie and Butch
were grinning and bopping in
their seats.
When the show was over
the boys walked us home, down
past the high school.
Carol and I were dancing ahead
– still melting from Elvis.
Butch grabbed Carol's arm
and they headed behind the
school. Ronnie spread his
jacket on the ground and
we sat. His lips were on mine,
my mind was on Elvis. Then
my skirt was up, Ronnie was pushing
I felt a pain, and I jumped up and
ran home, blood streaming
into my bobby socks. I dodged
my Mom, scrubbed my body, and
pretended to go to sleep. When
everyone was in bed, I went outside and
buried that orange and white skirt.

DISCOVERING WHAT'S IN THE CLOSET

CRANBERRY RED SILK VELVET DRESS

Genesis.
The dress refuses to be
replicated, supplanted, replaced.
There will never be a substitute
for that first taste of luxury.
Suddenly at four years old I
outgrew it. And Mom gave it away.
Away! I still wanted it.

Psalms.
I find myself writing
long songs to garments, pieces of
silk, satin, taffeta. Rarest bits
of grosgrain, tissue thin lawn,
bloodied wool. Remembering my Sunday
undies, my Platex girdle in minty green
that held my already flat stomach flatter.

Acts.
Before I learned to read I raised my
homemade dress in church and proclaimed:
my slip has my name on it! the cotton
garment read: PILLSBURY. Three years later
I wore my favorites to school: a
drop-shoulder blouse and full circle
skirt made from our living-room
curtains and slipcover castoffs.

Lamentations.
My father died. Mom stopped
making my clothes and started making
step-fathers instead.

Revelations.
Deep pockets of lies lay in
wardrobes filled with cocktail dresses and
platform sandals with long narrow straps
made for a princess who couldn't provide
school shoes for her daughters.

MOM'S WHITE STRAPLESS DRESS: A 50'S MEMOIR

Shimmering as moonlight
on a lake at three A.M.
layered as a bride's cake
with your skirts of net
and lace and acetate,
you embrace her bosom,
cinch her waist, then
soar nearly to the floor
stopping to admire her
dainty ankles – like everyone
else in the room.
Me, I have my eye on you,
for I have plans.
You and me, baby.
We're going places.
To the prom, for starters.
I'll add two crinolines
and a wrist corsage.
Then for the spring concert
I'll be demure, and
wear a blue bolero
and blue satin pumps.
You'll still be the
star of the show.
Let's think pink
for graduation.
I'll tie a ribbon in my hair
and one around my waist.
I'll use them to hang you
on the tree by the lake –
in the moonlight
at three A.M.

CUBAN HEELS

We were so dangerous then
with our Cuban heels and our
toreador pants. We were. If
we spoke our minds, or
asked for the same pay or
even the same jobs as men.
Those same clothing items today
are called kitten heels and capris!
So playful and carefree
not bloodthirsty, not
political, not even
risky. The pants –
though they're tighter –
are 10 percent lycra.
And the heels are still
a mere couple of inches
off the ground. We
tiptoe around our
independence now the
same way we did fifty
years ago – in lipstick,
cashmere and falsies.
Our granddaughters
wear falsies on their
eyelids as well as on
their chests and count
it as liberation that no one
cares. We are free to
swear and work the
same hours as men
for slightly more on
the dollar than we did
thirty-five years ago.
We don't have equal rights,
but if we are brave enough
we can make complete fools
of ourselves.
So, kittens, kick up
your Cuban heels!

THE RIGHT FOUNDATION

Every day when I carried
the money drawer to the
drive up window
you waited for a quick
feel.
I was in training
I was going to be
a real bank teller
a man's job.
If I complained
I would lose my chance.
I'd seen what happened
behind the teller windows
to Frankie, the other
woman teller, Vern's
hand on her ass.
You slid your hand
under my dress
above the stocking
reaching for the
sweet spot.
I needed this job.
I deserved this job.
We were required
to wear stockings,
dresses or skirts,
slips, girdles, not
too much jewelry.
I went shopping.
I bought a new girdle.
A rubber Platex
to wear over panties.
Two pairs of panties.
And a sanitary pad.
Every day of the month.
When you frowned, I
shrugged.
Platex was the
right foundation.

QUICKENED
Mothers are always right.
Life does not have to be a tragedy. - Felicia Mitchell, <u>My Turn Out of The Box</u>

You throw the rat poison
bottle out the door, down
the hall. It doesn't break.
By the time I retrieve it
see the skull and crossbones
you have barred your door
and gone silent.
Scared, crying, but tiptoeing
I run outside the house,
peer in the windows for
a glimpse of your dying body
or maybe your prankster self
having a good laugh on me
like I thought you were
when Dad died.
That was no joke. Is this?
I can't take it no more
you said before you
slammed the bedroom door
and sealed your promise
with a tossed vessel.
A darkened room, no
sound. Do I dare call
for help, risk your wrath
in exchange for my peace of mind?
Just because I wish you dead
doesn't mean I want to be an
orphan. Do you really want to
die? Isn't drinking enough?
I'm 14, I don't know. Sometimes
I want out pretty bad myself.
I call your aunt and uncle.
No answer. I take this as an
omen, that no call is
necessary. In the morning
you slide the dresser away
from your door and are
resurrected.

THE PRINCESS AND HER PRINCES

When the sun went down the princess
went to her wardrobe and flung open
its mirrored door.
Inside were dresses sparkling
in the colors of my old Crayola box:
aquamarine, burnt sienna,
deep ruby red.
My favorite were the two
opposites: bridal white
and black taffeta.
Shoes to match every dress
and the extra dove gray platforms
with crossing 12 inch straps
just because
she had small feet and
tiny royal ankles.
She displayed all her
best assets in these
garments and accessories.
Every Friday and
Saturday night the
witch went dancing at the
Silver Star Tavern
with a handsome prince
who upon closer inspection
resembled a warty toad.
A sweating, rotten-breath amphibian
who promised to get me a
singing contract.
Or the other one who said
I had bedroom eyes.
Our fridge was empty,
my shoes had holes,
the princess witch and
her princes wore raiment
of kings with pockets
full of promises
which upon closer
inspection resembled
crumpled bits of fabrication.

DISCOVERING TEEN MARRIAGE

ABOUT A BRUISE

That first bruise he gave me
should have sent me running
looking in another direction
for my way out of my mother's
house.

It was 1959. Summer in a
tiny town in Missouri. I wanted
out and I couldn't survive another
three years. I had a sort of plan. If
I got pregnant I could go to a
home for unwed mothers. I could
finish high school and give up my
baby for adoption and go to work.
Never go back home.

There was a boy. He wanted me.
Our mothers were friends, so going
out with him was never a problem.
One night at the drive-in movie, I
didn't do something he wanted me
to do. Or respond quickly enough,
or answer in the way he thought I
should, and he had had a lot of beer.
So he grabbed my ear and twisted it.
Hard. For a long time.

The next day the top of my right
ear was blue black. And so sore I
gasped when I touched it. So, I
wore my hair down, in spite of the
mid-summer heat. And I never
said a word.

I OPENED THE DOOR

I opened the door and the wind came in

bringing every dirty trick you ever thought of
right with it … gathering under the table
ganging up in the corners trying for all
the world to look like innocent little
dust bunnies swirling around my

ankles pulling me flat on the
hardwood floor pulling the
rug out from under me when
I was carrying our son in my
nine-month belly or a

fresh-baked peach pie that first
Thanksgiving with your Mom and
brother, Aunt and Granddad all
looking on, watching the
peaches slide down the wall

six years that door stood open
while the tricks stacked up and
tumbled over tripping me every
time I hurried to soothe your
troubled daydreams landing in
another nightmare

until one night the police held
you back as I packed one bag and
quietly closed the door behind me.

SHOPPING SPREE

I went on a shopping spree
in 1965. You kidnapped our
son and refused to let me
see him. I begged, I
went to court where I
didn't even get to
have my day after
my witness didn't
show up. My witness
who was also my
mother decided to
work that day rather
than face you in
court, so our lawyers
met with the judge
and decided that as
you had the bigger
salary — surprise — and
the larger apartment
and your mother to
babysit our son that
despite your drinking
and violence and
kidnapping proclivities
you were the better
parent. I thought
maybe I needed a
better wardrobe so
I took my Famous and
Barr charge card out
for an afternoon
and spent five
hundred dollars.
Five hundred dollars.
Enough to buy a
car, two months'
salary, an entire
fall wardrobe. I
had the bill sent
to you.

UNREQUITED LOVE

Thirty years since you threw me
downstairs, locked me out after
three hours of slapping punching
mutilating as I pleaded not
in front of our son
still you telephone me
beg proclaim undying love
swear your life is crippled
by the pain of my rejection.

I would hang myself in the
stairwell rather than return the
emotion I spent thousands
of dollars and thousands
of hours in a whirligig chair
to overcome.
I can longer stomach a
contest to learn who
has the greater
threshold for pain.

Once more I've changed
my number, again
unlisted. Should you find
me, leave your message
and I will get back to
you. Never.

LIPS MOVING WHILE READING

I didn't love you, I never
said I did. I did pay you
the highest compliment I
knew: you smell like my
grandma. I once said that
when you were sweaty and
smelled of cigarettes and
held me close.

There were other times I
felt close, like when I
saw your lips move while
you were reading. That
reminded me of my grandpa
who struggled so mightily
to learn a few words of
the Bible. By then I'd
learned not to give you
compliments.

Now that your bones have
been resting up on that
hill a few yards away
from my grandma for nearly
twenty years, I wonder if
you are ready to forgive
me. I forgave you for the
physical abuse, even before
you killed yourself. Can
you forgive me for using
you as my way out of
town?

SHOTGUN MARRIAGE

He put the belt around my life,
— I heard the buckle snap,
And turned away, imperial,
My lifetime folding up ...
  Emily Dickinson

He didn't know better, he was as
trapped as I, and only three
years older. But he was the
man, the husband, the soon
to be father, and I was like a
caged animal, wildly longing
for my freedom. Time
tamed neither of us, but
eventually set us free.

MISSPENT MOTHERHOOD

i squandered my motherhood
mistaking it for my youth
believing that because i
was sixteen or twenty or
thirty i was entitled to
indulge in the activities of
youth.
scholarship, art, drinking,
unbridled sex.
dragging my children along
as if they were accessories
like pocketbooks
instead of easily bruised fruit
to be guarded from danger
tended like gardens
raised to be guardians
of the future –
of their own futures

i rushed into adulthood
as if it were the answer
instead of the quest.
and therefore i lost
my opportunity to grow
into being grown
up – until my own
children were nearly
grown themselves.
they grew like weeds – no
nurturing, no watering.
They are not weeds.
My children are
wildflowers.
i am their mother
however nonchalant
i may have been.

ALL THIS REMAINS
TO BE DISCOVERED:

I. At five:
why grownups take naps
where Mom hides candy
when I can touch myself
what makes me cry
who will ever love me

II. At fourteen:
how to pretend I'm just like all the other girls
when it's okay to call for help
how to avoid grown men's groping hands
who will ever love me

III. At twenty-nine:
how to start over
how to go to college as a grown-up
how to live on two-hundred a month
how to tread treacherous waters

IV. At thirty-three:
how to be a lesbian
how to start over
how to live

V. Later years:
how to accept love that is there
how to forgive and move on
how to live gracefully
where to hide my candy, and
how to start over ...
again.

DISCOVERING MYSELF AS A LESBIAN

DON'T SPEAK

Don't say a word, just
close your eyes, part
your lips, and let me
hold your head in my
hand as my lips touch
yours and my tongue
brushes your teeth
seeking to silence
you for another
moment, give me
another brief
interlude for the
story that lives
in my body when
you are near me
that begins as
a heat rising
from my center
a breath quickening
my pulse racing
my ears straining
to hear our hearts
beating in unison
my thighs reaching
for yours even when
I'm still seated
still driving to
our destination the
hair on the back of
your neck calls the
palm of my hand
like a magnet to a
pin. I'm helpless.
Let our warmth guide
us. No need for
words.

IN THE DARK

Everything you ever say
in the dark I say in
the daylight but that
sends you scurrying
like a silverfish
for your moldy book
or a thick new tome
never willing to
face the poetics
of the night in the
light of the day.
Under the moon or
the starless velvet
skies I hear your
silken or hoarse
whispers of desire
flattering phrases
describing my limbs
my skin, my moist
proof of yearning
for your touch. When
I am moved to sing
these same psalms
in the morning rays
to you, to your
neck, your shoulders,
your smell, that
place you called
your bathing suit
area when we were
children together…
you need to read
and I am left to
sing my aria to
the window above the
sink as I make our
morning tea.

HOW TO INFLUENCE DREAMS

Say you love me, court me
sweep me off my feet
dance with me, make me laugh
dress up, be cool, do something
I can't do for myself.

Make me moan with longing
sing to me, whistle for me
bake me a cake.

Buy me presents and tell me
I look pretty. Be unable to
gaze at any other woman
when you're with me.

Smell good, have sweet lips
and a hot crotch. Bump and
grind with me, then kiss
me sweetly and say you'll
see me later.

Call me, text me, send me
an email when I least
expect it. Bring me
balloons. Wake me up at
midnight.

TUXEDO AND GOWN (BEAUTIFUL)

We were beautiful the day
we went to the prom. The
gay and lesbian prom took
place on June 15, 1984. You
rented a tux, I bought a
vintage gown and let out the
seams. We both had the
loose curls of romance, and
the pink bloom of youth.
Your photographer friend
came to the house and
took professional shots of
you, me, us, my cat, our
flowers, piano, and the
sun streaming in the windows.
You were slim, handsome
in your white shirt, black
tux, cummerbund and tie, I
was voluptuous and beaming
in shell pink tulle, white lace,
rose pink taffeta with satin
undergarments that made
seductive music when I walked.
We look like newlyweds in
that stack of photographs.
There is a shot of our hands
in white-gold filigree rings with
expensive stones, holding hands,
though we were never wed,
only divorced after nineteen
years. On prom day we
were beautiful.

NOTES AND CREDITS:

CRANBERRY RED SILK VELVET DRESS
Performed by VOX Chorus, 2011

DON'T SPEAK, Invert Sugar, Binge Press, 2012

IN THE DARK, Invert Sugar, Binge Press, 2012

MISSPENT MOTHERHOOD was published in
Mother Egg, Volume 9, May 2011.

*MOM'S WHITE STRAPLESS DRESS: A 50'S
MEMOIR* was published in the premiere issue of The
Stillwater Review, 2011.

HOW TO INFLUENCE DREAMS was published in
Lavender Review, Night Issue, June 2011; Invert Sugar,
Binge Press, 2012.

Author photograph by Beverly Standish

Cover photograph by author

Made in the USA
Monee, IL
07 July 2026